73

Every Little Vanishing

 C8

by Sheleen McElhinney

Write Bloody Publishing

writebloody.com

First edition.
ISBN: 978-1949342215

Cover Design by Lily Lin
Interior Layout by Winona León
Edited by Jeremy Radin
Proofread by Wess Mongo Jolley
Author Photo by Lori Ann Brunetti

Type set in Bergamo.

Printed in the USA

Write Bloody Publishing
Los Angeles, CA

Support Independent Presses
writebloody.com

For Michael

EVERY LITTLE VANISHING

Every Little Vanishing

To A Brother

Sure, you were messy. Drank from the measuring glass,
ate off the cutting board, littered the bathroom floor

with powdered dime bags, singed spoons—
wept on the carpet, puked on the carpet, went on

and on about how you'd get better, never got better.
Sure, I lost sleep. All those nights you stayed out—

and I'd ask some imperceptible god above
my bedroom ceiling to carry my sharp

whisper to your ear, wherever you were—
under a bridge, a bathroom stall, a sunken

soiled cushion, clouded utopia—to wake up,
remember me. Come home.

I am selfish. I would take you in your suffering
over this grief that has replaced you.

It is a gnarly pit in the center of a whole tender life,
wasted. It is the ghost of you, throwing stones

at my bedroom window to let you in after dark.
Wants only to talk about the good times, us as children,

my brother, painting the nails
on my right hand, first boy to call me pretty.

It wants to play all your favorite songs on loop
so I can watch you dance forever down the long hall

of my memory. Watch you roller skate
backwards on the Palace rink.

Just when I think it's gone, it shows up
in the features of the nephew you never met. Eyes

the same forget-me-not blue. It is the crack
in the foundation of my house. Gets wider,

opens like a chasm, calls to me—
the lonely echo, where

everything I've lost has gone.

"Hell of a damn grave. Wish it were mine."

—*The Royal Tenenbaums*

ANOTHER NIGHT WOUNDED

He's dead. My God,
wake up, your brother is dead.
My mother hovers
over me, drooling tears, drooling
snot, heart like a flickering match.
The car outside of the house
is on fire. We run to the window,
press our hands to the glass, watch
the crackle and pop of burning
steel. Flames lick the sky
into wounds. My mother moans
like a tree in a storm. The cops come,
the firemen, the neighboring house
lights flick on. The neighbors whisper,
he's really done it this time. Dogs bark
on their chains, a growling to open
the charcoaled earth to let my brother
fall in. The car is empty. A singed shell,
a glowing coal. My skin turns
to ash, my lungs expand to bursting.
My feet pound the stairs
to his room, kick the door wide,
and there he is, this miracle
I prayed for, let him be alive,
slipped in from the open window,
blacked out in a pile of sheets,
face covered in soot, we are
another night wounded,
another night blessed.

It Wasn't Sad

that it was my fourth birthday, my doll body
smocked in blue taffeta, white tights
sagging at the knees. There was a cake,
a song, maybe balloons. It wasn't sad

that I stuffed myself into a closet hoping
they'd come looking, a full length mirror propped
against the wall, golden base kissing
the toe of my patent leather shoe. It wasn't sad

that the mirror fell, shattered into hard rain
sharp enough to cut through flesh. That
I could've been screaming but all I saw
was blood and bone. It wasn't sad

that the grown-ups were having fun, too,
their stale breath yeasting my face
as they flapped my skin back into place, wrapped
my body in a blanket and, drunk, drove me

to the hospital. It wasn't sad that they strapped
me to a bed, said big words like severed, big
words like artery. It wasn't sad. They said
I was lucky. Lucky for my life,

my one beautiful life.

CANDY SHOP (BOYS WILL BE BOYS)

The candy from the penny jar
    is only a penny, so me and Marcy

fill our pockets with copper,
    giggle our way through the shortcut,

already feeling the burn of a red hot,
    the melt of a cherry ring pop. The boys

in the parking lot, feasting
    on their own hearts like scraps of raw meat.

They poke the wet lining of their cheeks
    with bottle stiff tongues, jerk an invisible rope

with gummed up hands, grind
    their hips against the hissing space between us.

They moan our girl names in cursive
    and tell us to kiss like our mothers.

I grab Marcy's hand, we knock our knees, guard
    our pennies like diamonds.

Revenge Scene

Okay, picture this: We're in an elevator.
The elevator shuts down. It doesn't matter
where we're going, only that we're alone.
My inner child presses the buttons until
they all glow. He eyes the Emergency pull
and I shake my head no. This time, I'm
in control. I am the shapeshifter. I am the
human grotesque. I grow larger in this
space, loom over him like a bad dream,
watch him piss his pants. Then I peel off my
clothes and shrink down to my 11 year old
self, unbudded breasts, undarkened nipples,
a pale bubble gum pink. He recognizes me
now. I stick out my tongue and a movie
plays on its fleshy surface; not the rape
scene, but after. All the new names I was
given, my own mother stiffening her back,
taking away my dolls. I don't cry. I gush a
river of blood. The elevator reeks metallic,
fills up past his manhood, up to his gaping
mouth and chokes him. But I'm okay—I
know how to hold my breath.

Halloween 1991

I wear a giant paper mâché head
over my human head.
A lumpy globe molded
by my mother's hands.
My older siblings a flurry
of chatter and flammable
fabric just within earshot.
I am top heavy but no one
can see my blonde curls, my big
stupid doe eyes. I am alone
with my breath, the muffled
swoosh of a heartbeat in my ears
like I'm back in the womb,
which is the next best thing
to being dead. I can say
whatever I want and no one
will hear me. Like, *I think*
there's something wrong with me.
Or, *I don't think I like myself.*
I can't see out of the finger poked
holes, too high above my vision.
I lift my small hand to paw
at the dark and hope that someone
will take it.

WITCHES OF WESTBROOK

I watched my sisters,
    each of them trailing familiar scents
        like Oil of Olay, eucalyptus,
            like brushfire, like smoke.
        Watched the pale moonstone glow
    of their skin brown in another year
of sun, and another. Watched their love
    turn into swollen bellies, their arms turn
        into cradles. Watched the corners
            of their eyes grow lines like the pages
        of an open book. Watched them hurl
    fruit at leaving husbands, whip their hair
in defiance. I watched them lift their wet
faces to the next approaching storm, slip
    into new armors as unassuming as gossamer.
        I was so much younger. Their long lean bodies
            had stopped growing by the time
                I was born. They had already known
            the loss of a brother, gone
        before I arrived. Their small, smooth
    fingers tracing the blue satin lining
of his new lidded bed. Their hands opening
and closing his tin box of trinkets,
    Matchbox cars rusting in the salt from their
        eyes. They had felt the sprawling distance
            between the door and their father
                walking out, our mother tied to the bed
            to save her from herself, only waking
        for another heavy dose to take her back
    under, while they toiled, stared into an empty
pantry, learned to use the stove.
I still had a brother to love, then lose, my own
    hand to rest upon a frozen chest in the stillness
        of a quiet room. I still had children to birth, men
            to warm me and then leave me
                cold, heart to be crushed like a fig.

THE ILLUSIONIST
After Natalie Diaz

My brother was a regular Houdini;
thought himself invincible.
He said, *Watch me*
cloak myself in death's dark curtain,
then shake it loose, unscathed.

He practiced in his basement bedroom,
fifths of potent elixirs stuffed inside
hampers. I heard him screaming in the face
of the lion he was caged with, arms
covered in claw marks.

He stood before me, wild irises like the blue
of a flame, said, *Do you see me?*
Can anyone see me? I clasped his face,
thumbs resting in the hollows of his cheeks,
and watched him vanish like smoke.

I heard him sob when the odds
seemed against him. Watched him slink
inside a box to cut himself in half, head
like a bloated ball of cotton. Believed when he said
those syringes were just props

filled with water. He said much of the draw
was the feel of the needle, the prick
of a pin into flesh. Not to worry, it's all part
of the show. He brought in assistants,
always skinny, always blonde,

to slip the keys like a pill down his throat,
to fetch me when he went too far. He fashioned
costumes out of bed sheets
and rubber bands the circumference of an arm,
dyed them with blood,

sequined them with regret. But though he studied
all the tricks, learned the secrets
from the illusionists in his circle,
he wasn't a very good magician,
and he could've been so many things.

MOTHER IMPOSTOR

The faces
of my children
lure me
from bed
each morning,
where I wake
from another death,
another night spent
dreaming up scenarios
in which I fail
them: their toes
at the edge of a cliff,
I am the dark abyss.
My body
is a kaleidoscope
of all the life
it's held,
each child
a crystal shard
shook loose.
They don't know
the people I used
to be, how many selves
I had to slaughter
just to be
their mother,
all the skins I've shed.
Just this morning,
I walked out
of myself
like a discarded
bathrobe,
so I could cook
the eggs, pour
the juice,
become
again.

ELINORE, A PORTRAIT

My mother is Thanksgiving
dinner, the pulled neck
of the turkey thrown into gravy
for flavor. She is the swanky
house party, shrimp cocktail
and Manhattans. Crazy,
like Patsy Cline. The bite
of a ginger ale fizz
in my small nostrils, the burn
of Vicks VapoRub on my chest.
87 pairs of shoes piled
in the shower stall. Phone numbers
and cartoon eyes scribbled
on every piece of mail, a fridge full
of condiments. She is Avon
and expired Chanel #5 with no cap,
a glass shelf of samples and dust.
Red lips and nude
pantyhose, cinnamon hearts
and root beer barrels,
endless cups of tea.
She is the paper bag womb
that carried eight children, eight kites
without wind, tangled up strings.
Veneer smile and ruby talons.
Holy water in the hallway,
Jesus on the wall. Polaroid Mom
in a bathing suit,
mom on the hood of a car,
high arches, boxed black hair
like a haunted house and I am
the ghost who grew up there.

I Saw It Coming

The night my mother threw another one of her dinner parties / another one my brother and I were made to clean for / as the perfumed ladies filed in before their smoke trailing husbands / my brother emerged from the bathroom we were forbidden from using / the one with the good towels / soaps shaped like rosebuds and winged cherubs / we ate them as children because they looked like chocolate / poison wax in our teeth / he stepped out with a towel around his waist / a cloak of steam fizzing from his shoulders / sashayed into the kitchen / beads of water dripping from his hair / an unpredictable rain / as he bent with a smile to kiss the powdered cheeks of my mother's friends / *you're so handsome* they said / *oh, your Michael is so handsome* they said / he peered into my door where I sat reading / his eyes wide wet planets / I said what are you on / he said *magic mushrooms you want some* / It was a bad idea / I did it anyway / opened my palm / slapped it to my mouth / ground them in my molars / down my adolescent throat / on the concrete steps outside our house we pressed the bones of our arms together / elbow to elbow / rolled into and away from each other like magnets / moon to tide / tide to moon / laughed at the audacity of living / the audacity of dying / I went back inside when I pictured him cold in a church and it wasn't funny / I stood in the kitchen / my eyes wide wet planets / my parents clinking glasses against their teeth / slurping cold shrimp from their lifeless tails

HONEYSUCKLE

When the house was too much, the lace curtains
like haunted brides in the windows, secrets
seeping through the floorboards—

someone's too young to be pregnant, someone's
on drugs, someone's fist made a crater
in the moon gray door, someone's drunk

husband is lying in the open dishwasher—
I would go outside, pluck the honeysuckle
from the honeysuckle bush, nip the bud

where the stem met the flower and slide
the frail shaft of its center past the buttermilk
petals and down the trumpet of its body

where the scarce nectar hid like God.
Ever so careful, ever so gentle, so as not
to snap the head from its neck

before it could give itself to me.

Take Me Back To The Church Basement

Rows of Formica tables and cold
metal chairs. Brown paper lunch bag stained
translucent from a wet tuna sandwich on pizza day,
white button down blouse yellowed from dog piss.
Let me take a big bite, climb on the table
and shout,

                You can laugh all you want.
It's okay to be like me, uncombed hair, no money
for the book fair. Some of you will die soon!
I've been to your memorials, I've lit candles
for you. Some of you won't be so lucky and life
will come for you, same as me, you precious little shits.
I know you now, your white picket fences. Listen,
some of you marry the wrong man, some of you have cancer,
and no, I wouldn't wish it on you. Some of you have gambled
your family away. Some of you will lie about whose child
it is, some of you will drink 5 stools down
from me at Carmen's Place and we'll share
a taxi home. Some of you, like me, will lose
the only people you love and it won't matter
if your parents pressed your uniform and gave you a crisp
dollar for a slice of cafeteria pizza. Someday, you'll think
of me and wonder if, against all odds, I made it.
You tell me.

I Don't Know Why It Matters

but when I was a kid
I picked up a dead
opossum from the side
of the road by its tail
and felt gravity pull
its bloated body back
to a sticky wet mound
on the gravel until I was left
holding the shelled skin
in my hand like a limp
and hollow sleeve.

I carried it, my untied
shoes shuffling under
its shadow, its coarse
hair matted with blood,
its mouth agape
in a vacant cry, to lay
it down in its last
animal summer...

That was my first
time holding
the dead. I knew then,
once the body
is cold, it does not come back,
even if no one is
watching.

LOVE IS PAIN

My brother left a note.
It was not addressed to anyone.
A reminder to himself, for all we knew.

Everyone wondered if he died
on purpose or by accident as if it would mean
something different.
He'd been killing himself his whole life.
There are things you cannot take back.

The girl he got pregnant, she aborted the baby,
he cried and said it was his fault—
a kid, he'd aimed a BB gun at a rabbit,
pulled the trigger, a litter
of tiny mewing mouths
falling from its tender insides.

MY SON

His scalp smells gamey / like a cut of meat / I guess that's what my genes smell like mixed with his father's / a sweating rack of lamb / I watch him at the table / gobbling down rabbit stew / his breathing heavy and labored / as if he hasn't been fed in days / His arm guards his food against invisible predators / He looks like a stranger to me / The thick mop of dusty brown hair / the wide nose / the growling and grunting / I bring the rug outside / hang it over a tree and beat it with a branch / watch the dust particles swirl and float in the sun / My hands are dry and cracked / an old woman's hands / When my boy was born / they were soft against his cheek / soft inside his curling locks of hair / still he suckled on my breast like a ravenous wolf / always taking more than I could give / His father doesn't know what he is / but I do / I lie in the dirt and wait / I sing softly to myself as the moon rises high in the night sky / A coyote howls in the distance / I'll be out here all night / waiting for my son to come home / and curl up in my skirt / weeping for all he's destroyed

The FedEx Man Always Knocks Twice

How many times have we been here, closing the door
against the outside as if we are prey, as if we are worthy
game, a prized head to hang on a wall, glass eyes
reflecting the hunter's face? It's not your fault.
Just last week a woman was murdered in a park nearby.
She was going for a run. She was running before running
meant not dying. It's not your fault. Once, you were crouched
behind a bush til dark, shook from the guts out, while a man
slapped a pipe in his open palm, softly singing *Here, kitty kitty*
over the crunch of his boots. When you were 13,
the man working on your house was caught peering into
the window of your second floor bedroom as you towelled
yourself dry and looked for all of your vanishing underwear.
Your brother, when he was still alive, still here to protect
you, sat on the roof with a shotgun waiting
for that same man to come back around because brothers know
what men are capable of. Once, you accepted a gift in exchange
for rape. Once, a man who offered you a ride home drove you
to his house instead. Once, you left your drink unattended, woke up
in the backseat of a car full of sleeping girls and you could only save
yourself. You have seen your own funeral so many times. You have
clutched your throat over and over with your own hands just to protect it
from someone else's. Sweetheart, the man at the front door—
he is just delivering a package, he is just conducting a survey,
he is just here to check the meter. You know so many good men.

ARCHAEOLOGIST OF FLESH

I would have called it a great
love affair if he had loved me back.

But it was all afternoon delight
and evening broom closet.

It's funny now to think the sound
of a zipper in its slow descent,

the teeth opening like jaws
to reveal the wet mouth of longing

was what I called love. How potent
the body that beckons, how tragic

to have made myself a landscape,
to have made his hands the tools

for digging, archaeologist of flesh,
to have hoped that somewhere deep

inside me, past the damp petals,
in the flowering earth of me,

he could have found something.

Whatever I Could Have Been

My son comes to my bedside,
a wordless calf.

I lift the corner of the duvet.
Every soft part of me awakes.

No matter what I say, there is
only this. I am nothing

but his mother.

THIS IS HOW I KNOW

My mother lost a child, two, three children
and she's still living. Her milk-drained
breasts still scooped into a department
store bra. Still goes out, orders the steak.
She says she had to stay alive for her other children,
for me. To watch me grow in her wilted
garden where the others could not.

I have a child, two, three children that hang
from me like streamers, reliant on
my wind. Gathering the linens from their small
beds, a bundle of threadbare dreams and angel sweat,
I could breathe them in forever. My youngest,
bashful under heavy lashes says *so much*,
because *I love you* is too hard to say. I imagine
my children gone, tiny caskets, abandoned toys,
a nightlight of stars swept across a vacant room.
Who would I be without someone to keep alive?
Without someone to mispronounce the word *love*?

My mother presses her parchment skin
to their supple cheeks, closes her eyes, glows
like a paper lantern. This is how I know
who I would be without these children to keep alive,
would be who I've been all along. A child
to keep a mother from dying.

May Fifth

I have moments of joy, I do.
When the wind blows the curtain
across the landscape of my body.

When I'm so busy loving
I forget I'm alive. Today you are
dead again on your birthday.

I am baking you another cake.
Eating it alone.
Singing for no one.

THE WOODPECKER

Maybe my mother is right
and I should see a doctor
about my depression.
But which one of us noticed
the woodpecker? Its tiny brain
bashing around its skull
like a dinner bell. She wants
to talk about how to fix this,
my sleeping so much,
my failing marriage, how my
mouth is arranged on my face.
Have I tried praying?
Have I cut down on wine?
I'm wondering about the bird;
its fruitless hammering.
Does it know its own futility?
That there's an easier way to find
worms? That the earth is so soft
you can be buried in it?

THE RING

5 a.m. was too early to go to a job
but that's what I got for working
in a bakery and why I forgot
to wear gloves and baked my ring
inside a pie and got fired for it.
The ring was bought for a girlfriend
who broke up with you before
your shy fingers got the chance
to slip it on hers, so you gave it to me
instead, because sisters don't hurt
you like that. I can still see it glinting
in some vat of lemon curd, silvering
in the glow of an oven, it's amethyst
heart nestled in a sterling crown.
I wore it like a *fuck you*
to the girl who couldn't love you back—
and now that you're gone, I'd smash my face
into every pie on earth just to
find it and let it choke me.

12 Step Training Manual For The Call

1. When the phone rings, it will sound the same as any other call. Your reluctance to answer will tell you otherwise. Answer it anyway.

2. Sudden death is not quiet. Practice smashing dishes against the wall. Let the tea kettle scream. Start moaning *No* into the loud, guttural stillness.

3. Exercise your jaw. Open and close it while watching TV. When the call comes, the pain will need somewhere to go. Your jaw will thrust open against your will. Your mouth: the exit door.

4. Practice throwing yourself to your knees. Start somewhere soft like the carpet and work your way up to the hardwood floor where you keep your phone.

5. Get your affairs in order. Fill the gas tank, shower, eat three meals a day. This will prevent you from having to make any unnecessary stops on your way to console friends and family.

6. Padlock your liquor cabinet. Remember you come from generations of drinkers the length of a tightrope across the Atlantic and everyone falls in. Remind yourself that your brother wasn't a good swimmer and neither are you.

7. Set your alarm for various times in the night. Upon waking, you will have trouble distinguishing between your nightmares and reality. Whichever feels worse, that's reality.

8. Drive to your childhood home. The people inside will look like your parents but they will be cored like fruit. Their eyes, drained of color, will look straight through you. Seperate yourself.

9. If at all possible, go to the beach. Stand in the ocean and let the waves take you out. Do not resurface until you are sure you will drown. Repeat.

10. Take inventory of your limbs. This loss will feel like an amputation. Tell yourself they are all still there, still capable of standing, feeding you, brushing your teeth, throwing dirt onto a lowered box.

11. Talk about your brother daily, to everyone and anyone who will listen. They may get annoyed but you will need to say his name. This is all part of the training.

12. Most importantly, tell yourself that he is better off dead. Now say it again.

OMEN

My blood's been replaced
with cement. I've been here
before. I am my own
statue of grief. Goddess
of death, patron saint
of failing organs. My father
lies under my gaze, in the hum
and suckle of tubes laced
through him like embroidery
thread, and I harden. He dreams
my brother comes in through
the window to kiss him
on the mouth. One by one,
they vanish. I walk
home, trailing doves.

THE FEAR

It takes three days for brown liquor
to leave my body. Same for my father
who calls it "The Fear"— that eggshell
existence with the yolk sucked out.
The Fear is a dry socket, fractured skull,
rodent brain. Enough shame
to fill up a bathtub, dye the water sober.
It's the dirty mouthpiece of a pay phone,
loose tobacco in a pocket, bruise
of unknown origin. Keeps getting bigger,
turns the garish shades of a mood ring.
Picture show of mistakes made, flashbulb
faces of men I hope I didn't. Panties stained
the sticky Rorschach of regret. Yes, said through
a mouth full of sand. The Fear, a rusty wind chime
calling me home with the scrape of a hollow whistle,
car parked on the front lawn, door swung wide
like an invitation to climb back in
and drive to a bottle that quells it.

LET'S BE HONEST

It's that dream again.
The haunted attic.
Some forgotten dog
with buckling bones,
skull full of dents,
teeth emerging through
nipples, chewing
through its soft
underbelly. Something
eating it alive all this time
it's been locked away
with ghosts. I tell myself
it could mean a great
number of things—
but let's be honest,
I'm the dog.

Pity Party

My ex-boyfriends throw a party
when they learn of my divorce.
They invite my ex-husband, sit
wounded and buzzed around a fire.

They tell him it'll get better over time.
One day he'll meet a new girl, less
crazy, so much less than—but better.
They'll say soon you won't remember

her in your t-shirt, bleeding
through your boxer shorts, throwing
her leg across your junk
in bed. Her sweat,

the scent of her
greasy hair that woke you
from the waist down. A new
woman, docile and lilac-scented,

better. Someone like your mother.
They will spoon Ben and Jerry's
down their throats before they turn

on each other, wielding the spoons
as weapons. They're all the same,
these guys,

gouging each other's eyes out
until there's only one left
who thinks after all this time,

he can win back my feral heart.

PURGATORY

I want to hang a big painting on the wall
of this rented house but I don't actually want
to live here. These jaundiced rooms
the color of a dehydrated person's piss.

Catholicism talks about purgatory, some weak
and pallid realm between heaven
and hell, where I imagine bored ghosts
skip invisible stones across an invisible lake.

I think if they're right and purgatory is real,
you don't have to die to get there.
You can stand at the kitchen sink and eat a sad
sandwich. Some tasteless meat pressed

between the heels of God and the devil.
You don't have to be good or bad.
You just get the mail and there are no letters
or birthday cards, just past due bills

and flyers for missing people. It rains
all the time. If not then the sky is a cloudless
slab of drywall. You can skip a real stone across
a real lake and not even cause a ripple.

ORCHESTRA

This is a song we've heard before.
The young couple at the courthouse,
married out of necessity. The baby's

already born, rents all paid up.
We bought rings from a plastic
spinning rack the night before,

a 20-dollar dress from the mall.
Was it any wonder that years later
the dinner table would go quiet,

save for the tinny violin slice
of knife between fork, teeth grinding
through meat, wine sloshing down

the brass halls of our throats? I felt
there in the chill of that room, a wishless
coin fall into the well of my gut.

It sounded like a warning. *One day
you'll hear his last swallow like a concert pitch.
The plates clanking together, faucet*

*turning on. The orchestra of your failed
marriage. You, the conductor at the sink,
back turned to him, always.*

*He, the man in the front row
getting exactly what
he paid for.*

TUMBLEWEED

At the kitchen table—
    the low light hanging
        between us, the moths
            fluttering their talcum
                wings against the bulb,
                    the warm night breeze
                        slapping the screen door
                            in gentle applause,

    you're telling me something
        so funny I think I'll never
            forget it. It's so funny
                I cry.

What was it now?
    You're doodling on a napkin,
        some strange bird,
            maybe a cartoon
                man in roller skates,
                    or a portrait of me
                      with worms for hair,
                        or a tumbleweed for hair,

I can't remember.
    Our glass cups sweat
        into the fibers
            of the tablecloth.
                The clock moves its hands
                on the wall.

I don't know how long
    we sat there doing nothing;
        the wind sweeping across the tops
            of trees, chasing the night birds
                to the water that runs away
                    with my memory—I never
                      thought it'd matter.

You Get It

I don't want to pour myself a drink.
I don't want to buy myself something nice.

I am exhausted as an unhinged gutter
after a downpour. I am diagonal, a leaning
fence post in the wet mud.

Maybe it's motherhood.
Look at this world.
Every day it's ending.

LILY OF THE VALLEY

My brother's birth flower still blooms
without him, adorns the ground

in my parent's garden, sprouts up
through the sprawling pachysandra.

Tiny rungs of cotton bonnets,
belled baptismal gown, seeded rattle.

Now, dew-topped umbrellas
in a graveyard of ghosts,

milk-white skulls, frilled at the teeth,
heavy on the bent spine.

Swallow

O, the full bloom of petals I'd tear from the stem to devour.
O, the small birds from my window with their soft plumes.
I would pop them whole onto my tongue, gulp the silk
of their feathers into my belly where I grieve, fill myself
up with whatever the sun makes gleam to shed a light
into the well of my sorrow. O, my mother's garnet,
O, my father's gold band. I would slip the rosary beads
buried with my brother down the coffin of my throat.

I Cannot Love You Here

Not in the silence of your anger.
Not in whatever shape it is

you're holding onto inside
your fists. I know the children

are small. I know you've seen so much
of me. My body a mussel, shucked

for the pearls inside. Our beautiful
boys. How they look like us.

How they still will when I leave.
How I hope they'll turn out more

like you and less like the woman
who cannot love you, standing

in our kitchen, asking why.

WE NEVER

Our love was not loud.
We never threw lamps, never
upended the patio furniture
after locking each other out.
We never screamed or cried
or fucked the bed frame to splinters
in apology. We never said, *stay*,
don't go. We never said *coward*,
or, *bitch*, or *fuck you*,
or *please*. We never snuck
through the window or slammed
the car door or got inches too close
to bull's-eye pupils. Never wrenched
throats or yanked hair or murdered
each other or killed ourselves—

out loud. We did it all
so quietly, like the slow
ascent of my bare feet up the stairs,
high heels hooked through my thumbs,
closing our door whisper soft,
the quiet groan of my weight
in the bed, stiffening our backs
to each other, switchblade
shoulders brandished, slicing
the death between us, til silence
do us part.

THAT STUPID SONG

It was just a kiss,
        but it popped all the bulbs on the street.
        I didn't even know him,
            we were two strangers in a bar.
I told him it was my birthday
        and he sang that stupid song.

I studied his mouth
        like a foreign language. He studied mine too.
Watched it spool,
        purr velvet. I wanted to feel the hum
           of his blood on my lips.

Just once. And what I'm trying to say
              is that I'm married,
        and I wanted to be good. But I was never
kissed like that.
        Like a defibrillator shocking my lonely
              sex. Like I wanted
          to be sung that stupid song
          every year for the rest
               of my life.

Like my mother tongue
        is that kiss, in that bar,
           with a man I will never see
again, who will never know me,
        but whose mouth
        I will wish for
          when I blow
           my candles out.

STILL ALIVE

I look like my brother in all the ways
in which he was gaunt and tired.
In all the ways where you could tell
he was from a small town and grew up
on Cheese Whiz and Wonder Bread.
In all the ways where he was handsome
and didn't know it, hands stuffed inside
pockets around people with money.

He'd be so proud of me now, raising
all these kids, crying in the shower
like a broken baptism just to walk out new
and clean and doing the best I can.
I look like him when I climb the stairs
and catch a glimpse of myself in the mirror
on the landing, my skin like a loose garment,
but still alive, and so, still beautiful.

SIXTEEN

My daughter's laugh is mythical.
Formed in the belly of the earth.
Birthed under a pink starburst moon.

Upstairs, in a tangle of bubblegum
girls, a sauna of cucumber melon mist,
she tells the best jokes, she laughs

the loudest. A volcanic eruption
of pixie dust. She laughs a sonic boom,
wind chimes in a hurricane, sudden

as a brick through a window.
All those years she suffered,
with this and that, like most

girls do, moaning like a bell
in a tower. I don't dare
clean up the glass.

I SURRENDER

to the crusted pan, the burnt toast,
the chicken left out overnight.

To the crack in the windshield, the flat
tire on I-95. To the fevers, the vomit

spewing from my children's mouths.
To the black mold, the weeping faucet.

To the bill collectors, the splunk
of the phone in the toilet, the bird shit,

the antidepressants. To the gynecologist
cranking me open, dentist cranking me open.

To the stretch marks, middle-aged pudge,
new hairs glinting silver.

To my brain repeating a segment
from Oprah's super soul Sunday,

I am not a human being having a spiritual experience,
I am a spiritual being having a human experience.

To the hundred yellow carnations thrown
onto my father's grave, my high heels sinking

in mud. To the dead people I loved
not growing older so close to celebratory

barbecues, hot dogs and fireworks, dance
recitals and due dates and the birth of Jesus

Christ, I surrender.

THE THIRD BABY

The third baby slept at my breast
in our bed. Mouth like a silk purse
waiting for pearls. We bought a plastic
imitation Mason jar filled with artificial
fireflies, a speaker and dial we set
to ocean. We handed him back
and forth at midnight, at 2, at dawn,
when he shrieked us awake again
and again until we both turned to ash
in our skin. Until four months later
I left him at my sister's feet, drove
to the emergency room to sleep,
you by my side, pulling up my blanket
like a shield of down. We gave him
songs, we gave him sweet nothings.
We disintegrated like the wings
of a moth to please him,
the baby we swore we'd never have,
our marriage a bridge between staying
for the children we had or leaving
for the people we wanted
to become. The third baby asked us
to choose. We decided to give him
for better or worse:
everything.

SOMETHING LIKE LOVE

I hold their faces,
graze the peach fuzz
with my lips, inhale
their supple cheeks,
kiss their eyes, the corners
of their lips where milk
crusts. These children,
if they don't grow up
soon, I will gorge myself
on their youth, their plump
fists, their pale slender necks,
their sweet unknowing.
I watch them run from me,
squealing ahead of my shadow.
I catch their scent
and hunger for something
older than me. Something ageless.
Something like love.

You Will Still Be You

You'll move to a new house.
You'll learn the street signs:
Chestnut, Forsythia, Willow and Pine.

You'll crouch down and rub
the grass between thumb
and forefinger. Your feet will learn

the floorboards; this one creaks,
this one snags. You'll remind
yourself to fix the window

in the hall, the one that sticks.
The house will be old
and you'll like it. At first,

it will feel like thrift store shoes
on your feet. You'll paint
the walls whisper white,

your memories trailing
behind you like ghosts,
place your forgetting pills

behind the small mirrored
door above the sink. You'll lie
in the darkness with your lover

at your back, breathing *things
will be different* into the hairs
on your neck. But you will still

be you, waiting in stillness
for something soft to come
along. An invisible embrace

to keep the goodness in,
like a vase around
flowers, torn at the root.

Everything Is Temporary

It's December 21st. The world
outside my door is a frozen lake, snow tight
enough to walk on without sinking.

> In the womb of the tinted
> light fixture above
> my bathroom sink

is the shadow of a bee.
It's striped bulb body
pinging against the thin glass.

> Ping. P i n g. Ping.

I signed the rental papers
for this place a week ago
and every day there is a new bee.

> Crawling out from the
> floor vent, stitched to
> the arm of my sweater.

I'm sluggish with change.
The neighbors ask where I came
from. I came from here and I'm

> still here. Just on a
> different street.
> A new key on the ring.

I'm just older now.
My misery another
spider vein on the thigh.

> I don't care about
> the amenities. I won't go
> to the pool in summer.

Won't rent a grill for any
birthday parties.
Everything is temporary.

> I won't dispute
> the bees.

Ode To Finding Love

If this is a love story, I can't hear it.

Not over the sound of my own heart

guarding its queen.

I do not yield to fingers tucking

a flower behind my ear. I do not

blush a pink burn. I do not downcast

my eyes for anyone.   But you—

I am ashamed. I find empty containers

ready to be filled with reasons

to live. I shop for dresses

that expose my spine to lure you here.

I could unzip my skin like a dress

and point to the buzzing,

a hive of bees making honey

in the organs for you.

The quick pulse of it,

a shimmy of blood to the body.

Oh, my wrists, oh, my neck—

that quiet tender bleating.

No matter it's been here before

in the shape of a man's shadow.

No matter it left like a man.

I am still worthy, I say.

Come to me.

My arms have nothing to hold.

LET IT GO

A tree with severed branches
is still a tree. An empty
vessel, still a vessel.
If it is shame brought to light,
every mistake you swallowed
like torn and crumpled
newsprint, let it burn
up the chimney of your bones.
You perfectly imperfect
body, you disappearing sun,
receding wave of froth, dark
winged bird growing small
on the horizon, your ghosts
a whisper in the rearview.
You have been broken so you
can put yourself back
together, eyes growing softer
with every little vanishing.

MAYBE

Maybe it's this.
    A new bird. Brilliant
        streak across the sky.

My three-year-old
    on his harmonica.
        The good honey pooling

slow on my spoon.
    Those lilac blooms,
        that midnight oil iris.

Clean sheets and smooth
    legs, ice in my glass, peaches
        bathed in a bowl of cream.

And did you hear
    that new song? It doesn't
        remind me of anyone.

I didn't think
    they wrote songs
        like that anymore.

Acknowledgments

Thanks to the editors of the following journals where the following poems, or earlier versions of them, first appeared:

Dogzplot:
My Son

Poetry Is Currency
Purgatory
The FedEx Man Always Knocks Twice
The Woodpecker

Sledgehammer Lit
We Never
On Finding Love

West Trade Review
The Illusionist

Abandon Journal
Revenge Scene

Poetica Review
Everything Is Temporary

Hole In The Head Review
I Surrender
To A Brother
Swallow
Maybe

Capsule Stories
Halloween 1991
Witches of Westbrook

HEARTFELT THANKS

To Megan Falley, teacher/poet extraordinaire, whose unwavering belief in me is the only reason this book saw the light of day, and without whom I would still be screaming into the void. To Jeremy Radin, legend, editor and performance coach of my dreams who taught me that *fear is just excitement in a monster costume*. To Derrick C. Brown and the Write Bloody team for choosing me and giving my book a home. To Riley Cowing, whose friendship and encouragement sustained me in the pursuit of this dream, and to the wonderful community of poets I have met along the way. To my family, for graciously allowing my truth to exist in the world. To my father and brother for their support from the other side. And to you, my readers—thank you, thank you, thank you.

ABOUT THE AUTHOR

SHELEEN McELHINNEY is a poet, baker, robot maker born and raised in Bucks County, Pa., where she currently resides. She grew up in a large family and has three astounding children of her own. This is her first book.

If You Like Sheleen McElhinney, Sheleen Likes...

Drive Here and Devastate Me
Megan Falley

Slow Dance with Sasquatch
Jeremy Radin

Racing Hummingbirds
Jeanann Verlee

Atrophy
Jackson Burgess

Our Poison Horse
Derrick C. Brown

Write Bloody Publishing publishes and promotes great books of poetry every year.
We believe that poetry can change the world for the better. We are an independent press
dedicated to quality literature and book design, with an office
in Los Angeles, California.

We are grassroots, DIY, bootstrap believers. Pull up a good book and join the family.
Support independent authors, artists, and presses.

Want to know more about Write Bloody books, authors, and events?
Join our mailing list at

www.writebloody.com

WRITE BLOODY BOOKS

CPSIA information can be obtained
at www.ICGtesting.com
Printed in the USA
FSHW011943270921

9 781949 342291